My Nonna's Boo Boo

A Lung Transplant Story

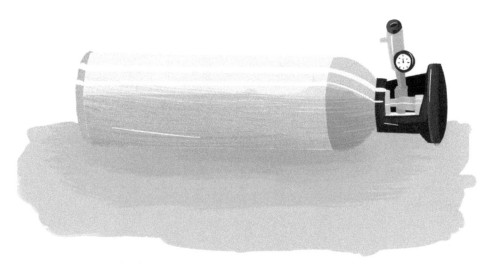

Written by A. Goddard
Illustrated by Kholis Je

My Nonna's Boo Boo by A. Goddard.

Second Edition.

Published by Lucky Frog Productions.

www.agoddardwriter.com
www.facebook.com/AGoddardWriter

For permissions contact:
ash.goddard27@gmail.com

Art by Kholis Je.

Ebook ISBN: 978-0-692-04362-9
Soft Cover Print Book ISBN: 978-0-692-04362-2
Hard Cover Print Book ISBN: 978-0-578-40525-4

This book is dedicated to
my mom and my son.
I love you more than you know.

My Nonna had a boo boo.
Her lungs were hurt and sad.
She saw some special doctors,
to help her not feel bad.

She started to get sicker.
She moved a little slower too.
She even had special air,
so she could play and say, "I love you."

One day she went to a new place.
They said they had a surprise.
An Angel lost their life today, to give her
lungs that were the perfect size.

She went away to get them fit.
Oh how perfect they would be.
Soon she would be home again,
and she would play with me.

Mommy went with her
and she stayed a little while.
She told me she'd be home soon.
She couldn't wait to see my smile.

Mommy said Nonna's new lungs
were working extra hard.
They had to settle into their new home.
They had so many things to do!
Like unpack their toys, shoes, and comb.

I got to see a picture of my Nonna.
She looked like she didn't feel so good.
I couldn't wait to give her a great big hug
to make her feel better.
My Nonna would love it!
I knew she would.

I had to wait patiently for
the doctor to say it was ok.
But I finally got to see my Nonna.
So I jumped and cheered.
"Hooray!"

I told my Nonna all the things
I wanted to do with her.
Like swim, visit the park, or just play!
She smiled and said,
"I promise we will do all those things.
I promise we will someday."

I didn't understand.
Her lungs were fixed and new,
but my Nonna still couldn't play with me.
There were so many things
I wanted to do!

She smiled and kissed
my head real soft.
She whispered in my ear.
"Don't worry. We'll have great
adventures soon my dear."

Mommy held me tight.
She ran her fingers through my hair.
She started to tell me what was
happening inside my Nonna, and how the
lungs were the perfect pair.

She told me about the special police in our body, called the white blood cells.
They were making sure her new lungs would fit in perfectly as well.

When the lungs moved into their new home,
the police decided to stop by.
Mommy said they had to check them out and
make sure they weren't a bad guy.

The Police were very happy.
They said the lungs were welcome to stay.
That meant the neighbors could come visit
them, since the Police said they were okay.

Mommy said I would have to be real
patient while Nonna's lungs got comfy in
their new neighborhood.
"Will they make new friends, Mommy?"
She smiled and told me of
course they would.

She said if I could hang in there,
for just a little longer, my Nonna
would come play with me.
She'd be so much stronger.

I waited and I waited.
My patience grew and grew.
Until one day I saw my Nonna.
She was so strong!
She was like brand-new!

Her lungs had made new friends.
They would dance and play every day.
I was so excited to see my Nonna.
We would finally get to play!

We played at the park. On the Swings,
Slides, and Monkey Bars too.
She helped me when I fell down,
and even found my shoe.

Now I get to have my Nonna with me, each
and every day.
All because a special Angel shared their
life that day.

Note from the Author:

I wrote this story to explain to my son what was going on with his grandmother. He was starting to ask a lot of questions, that I couldn't seem to answer quite right. I wrote the book, and had it drawn, so he could see what I was telling him. I wasn't expecting it to work so well, and to help other children as much as it did. I hope this assists you through the process of an organ transplant, like it did for my son.

CPSIA information can be obtained
at www.ICGtesting.com
Printed in the USA
LVHW072248011219
639096LV00022B/321/P